SHOULD YOU LOSE ALL REASON(S)

SHOULD YOU LOSE ALL REASON(S)

Justine Chan

CHIN MUSIC
P R E S S

BOOK AND COVER DESIGN BY Dan D Shafer

ISBN 978-1-634-05045-6

LIBRARY OF CONGRESS CONTROL NUMBER 2023933229

PRINTED IN Canada / First printing 2023

PUBLISHED BY Chin Music Press
1501 Pike Place #329 / Seattle, Washington 98101
www.chinmusicpress.com

Chin Music Press is based in the traditional territory of the Coast
Salish People, the Duwamish (dxʷdəwʔabš), in land that touches
the shared ancestral waters of the Suquamish (dxʷsəq̓ʷəb), Tulalip
(dxʷliləp), and Muckleshoot (bəqəlšuł) Nations. We honor the
people past, present, and future who belong to this place.

This publication contains reprinted samples of lyrics from the following:

For the land

For the coyotes

Let me tell you what it is like out here tonight.
Stories travel at night on the desert.
Someone gets in his pickup and
drives a couple of hundred miles for a
beer, and he carries news of what is
happening, back wherever he came from.
Then he drives another hundred miles
for another beer, and passes
along stories from the last place
as well as from the one before;
it is a network kept alive by people whose
instincts tell them that if they do not
keep moving at night on the desert
they will lose all reason.

—JOAN DIDION

Them old people used to tell these legend stories in winter. You can't sit down; you have to lay down; you can visualize them better. Also, I'll tell you, it's because you'll get a wrinkled ass. You don't want to be that way.

—CLIFFORD JAKE, INDIAN PEAKS BAND OF SOUTHERN PAIUTE

TABLE OF CONTENTS

SHOULD YOU LOSE ALL REASON(S)

WHY COYOTE LOOKS UP WHEN HE HOWLS

(A SOUTHERN PAIUTE WINTER'S TALE, AS I RETELL IT)

This story begins somewhere in the desert with a family of eight. There is a mom, dad, five daughters, and a son. They are very happy together.

One day, the dad gathers the family together and says, *I am very happy. But I'm very old and I'm very tired and I will die soon. And when I die, I want you to build a big brush pile and lay my body on it. Then, I want you to set the brush pile on fire—and then, run away. Run far, far away and do NOT look back. Whatever you do.*

So, when the dad dies, the family is really sad, but they do what they were told. They build that brush pile in the woods and lay his body on top. Then they set the pile on fire.

And it's all very frightening: the air is smoky and full of
crackling and the woods blaze red with the flames. The
mom and the daughters run away and don't look back.

But the son—and you can say that he was brave or dumb—
decides to look back.

And what he sees is that his dad is not dead. In fact, his dad
is sitting up and he's alive. Seeing his son seeing him.

And he is so furious.
He starts chasing his son.

The son runs and runs to catch up to the rest of the family.
He tells them, *Dad's not dead.*
He's alive.
We have to run. We have to hide.
If he finds us,

he'll kill us.

And so the family runs.

And so begins this long chase all through the desert. Even if the dad loves his family. No matter where the family runs, the dad can still follow their tracks.

They run and run.
When there is nowhere else to run, the son says to the family,
Let's jump up into the sky. That way we leave no tracks.

So the family jumps into the sky.

When the dad comes to the place where their tracks end, he cannot find them. He looks all around.

The son yells down, *Hey!*
Look up!

When the dad looks up and sees them, he is seething / boiling with rage. And for some reason, the family laughs at him and mocks him from up in the sky. He is too old to jump up.

Even more furious, the dad yells up, *If you don't come down from there, I will shoot you down!* And he grabs his bow and starts shooting arrows at his family.

Yet, in the sky, the family is more powerful now and they are
able to turn the arrows into little stars.

Finally, at this standstill, the dad says,
If you will not come down,
I will turn you into the stars.
And you can never come down again.

The son says,
But if we came down
you will kill us.
If you turn us into the stars,
we will turn you into the wild coyote.
Because you love this brushy country so much,
this is where you will live
and you can never come up.
You will run around the brush all night,
and when the day breaks and we fade away,
you will be very lonely.
You will be very sad.
You will look up at us and cry and yelp and howl.

And so it was so. And so it is now.
If you hear coyote howling and crying at the night sky,
it is because he misses his lost family.

THE END

(IF YOU) TURN US INTO STARS, (WE WILL) TURN YOU INTO THE WILD COYOTE

Because you always look back, you stand / on the stern watching the froth churn the arctic sea, white-tailed.

Because you always say the wrong thing—and still wish you could get away with more sass.

Because the shade always shifts with the sun, by the minute. Sifts through the cottonwood and velvet ash leaves.

Because you love the stories of dead things coming back to life—changed. Furious. Desperate. Inconsolable.

Because you can't stand to sit or stand to stand. But once the light has gone sepia, stand to run for hours in thunderstorms, lightning high on the ridge, drenched in rain.

Because with each day the sun rises later and sets sooner, and you are trapped / in the in-between.

Because you call yourself a desperado, think of your feet in boots strapped with shiny star spurs, dust on your soul, but you don't know the West.

Because, somewhere, nestled in the mountains, the only inland glaciers are melting and all you can do is look at the black-and-white pictures and ask where has it all gone.

Because you spend your nights watching for the moon, holding up your planisphere, lost. The paper doesn't match the sky.

Because the saudades tear at your throat.

Because you wish you were born in another time, another era, another place.

One version: you're in the middle of the sea, the crow's nest, reading the stars with astrolabes, drawing maps of uncharted territories. Your hands are rough and calloused from ropes, quick to tie strong knots. You love the rainforests, either temperate or tropical. You love the narrow inland passages, the threat of ice. You love the water, the salt. You are never seasick.

Because the air is so hot, full of rasping. The land so full of landmarks and stories you can't even begin to know.

Because you feel some part of you was / is / will always be secret.

Because the crickets are madness, a roar that fades to silence / if you forget / to listen.

Because you beg. You knock on doors. You don't know when to stop or how to begin. You are too young / too old for your own good.

Because, in the mornings, some thing cries / screeches helpless along the canyon walls. As if being torn apart by teeth or talons. A grey fox, that was, they tell you, but not why the sound.

Because you're always hungry / thirsty / weeping / raging / mad.

Because you love summer, the fever of it, the mind gone melty. The longest day of the year, the sun so searing / lined up with stones / everything. Solstice, but not the death of it.

Because you think in terms of saving or needing to be saved.

Because you once fell in love with a person, yes, but also, his stories / dreams of a desert. A desert of dormant volcanoes. Mojave tortoises. Joshua trees, their spines twining to the sky, under a cold moon. Miles of yellow flowers blooming for only two weeks of a glorious spring. Then, that emptiness.

Because, sometimes, the light gleams soft pink over basalt striped hills of iron oxidized green and straight cut mesas and cliffs. And you stand tall on a dirt road on the top of such a mesa and your bike tire is completely flat.

Because you are so afraid of being mediocre, of not being special. Of whatever glory your life holds is already behind you (and you look back).

Because the campfire smoke lingers in your hair, evergreen and juniper, and you lean into it.

One version: you're the folksinger in ratty denim and sundress. Hair sun-bleached red, ragged, and beachy. Brown-tinted sunglasses too big for your face. Riding shotgun in a lime-green Volkswagen van. Some melody always in your head, a harmony you can't get right. Every time you step out, whether it's at a gas station or in the middle of the desert, *Hello, world*. And the world wants you. You are wanted.

Because you're afraid of people leaving / believe that you need to be the one leaving / going / going / gone.

Because you think you know a place having been there a day or so. The streets, the people, the food. You like the siestas / the times when everyone else is asleep and you're out wandering / awake. Buzzed on sugary sangria and flamenco in a rowdy basement.

Because the doves, always unseen, make such wounded noises. And the crows are the same no matter where. And the wild turkeys run scaly-legged through the ferns like velociraptors, leaving shimmering square black feathers in their wake.

Because you are most cruel to yourself. Because you paralyze yourself.

One version: you lug around a typewriter in a suitcase, wear all black, gesture wildly when talking at parties, a lit cigarette always in hand. You read on the fire escape, jump into taxis. You call yourself—without that consciousness, that hesitation—a poet, and you actually write every day. If that's what it takes. You don't try to make anyone else happy and you don't care what anyone else thinks.

Because you don't belong here, up in the night sky, with the rest of us. You are not allowed to feel sorry for yourself.

Because, soon, winter will fall over the desert, snow soft on the sagebrush and manzanita trunks and baked lands. Because soon after, spring. And the snowmelt rush and waterfalls ephemeral. And the river will overflow its banks. The river will carry trees and boulders down. The river will take it all down. Because.

Because you love this brushy country so much, this is where you will stay / live / be. And you can never come up. You will run around the brush all night.

You will kick in your sleep. You will wake up cold.

You will be—you are—nobody without your uniform, without your hide. Bare / bear your teeth.

You will wonder about other wild deserts, with all their beautiful names—the Sonoran, Mojave, Great Basin—sprawling, bristling, untouchable. Read about them. Dream of them, their salt flats and sages, the rush of dried inland seas hollowing, hallowed. Dream of saguaro and tiny cottontails. Dream of cliff dwelling palaces in pale yellow sandstone at sunset, the light gauzy and faintly lavender. Hand and toe holds, ladders made of juniper trunks.

You will run and run until you run out of sweat and salt, and your hands go numb.

You will always feel not fully one thing or another but a matter / monster of failed fractions, strange chimera (come here) shaking.

You will stay still on earth while the stars tilt and the sun sallies round and your friends move away to the coasts.

The sacred datura will bloom, ghostly, through the night and smell so sweet (and there will be poisoned dreams).

Dream of dry invasive grasses wispy on mesas long after a summer burn. Dream of towering sandstone fins, the eyes of arches. Dream of bleached skulls and bones half-buried in sand. Dream of an infinite hazy and blue high, a life walking and dreaming along steep cut canyon cliffs, gullies, buttes, cattle paths, and ghost towns once hiding bandits.

You will always be late to the party and early to leave. In conversations, you will not know if people are talking with you or around you and would it be alright if you just walked away with your hands in your pockets.

At one moment, the mule deer will seem a rich light tan—the next, molted silvery and dark as the cottonwood trunks. They will edge out from the shadows, gather and feed on the freshly watered lawns all night.

You will befriend darkling beetles, bats, ringtails, tree frogs, American dippers, tiny lizards, prickly-pear cacti, mosses, and lichens. (They will not know what to do with you.) You will find humans increasingly strange, smelly, and idiotic.

You will always feel most yourself, turning the key in the ignition in a car you will never own and driving away on a dusty two-lane road cutting through chaparral / mesquite / alien canyon country red with iron, carved low by the water. The wide skies, and the horizon / infinite.

Almost all of your dreams will take place indoors / in a maze of a building. Sometimes, though, you'll find water and swim so easily.

You will see how far away you can get on just a bike and your two feet, coast along the highway and over an ancient metal bridge, past the cows, to the forgotten trails to the Eagle Crags, to an old Mormon ghost town. You will climb up on the ridge overlooking the cemetery and pretend you are the only one left in the world.

The river will always be cold / thrash muddy red in the monsoon rains.

You will want everything at once / and nothing at all.

No matter how cool the air, the sun will remain / a color / blinding, dried yellow, and harsh.

The quaking aspens will shiver their leaves to yellow and the streams of cold water will blur over long exposure.

You will stumble. You will swagger.

You will get used to never seeing the full red sun as it rises or sets. You will see peregrine falcons and turkey vultures circling overhead, but never the condors.

None of the pictures you take will be quite right. Not in focus. Or the light's not right. Or there is just too much.

You will bask. You will burn.

The bark of the spruce on the rim will always smell sweet and fresh in between its flaky scales.

The people will forget there was ever blanket poisoning of the public lands. That there are bounties for pairs of hacked off ears. That less, to rescind, must mean more.

You will think of water in terms of scarcity and abundance, in liters over hours, in mileages to the closest spring. You will miss the ocean.

You will be swift. You will be slow.

The sun will boil. The shade stay knife thin.

You will stand in stands of trees. The aspens, their dark whittled eyes watching you coax sulfuric water from the shallow spring into your water filter pouch. Neon blue dragonflies singe through patches of grass.

The wooden skeleton of the cableworks rigging will creak on the plummeting edge, trembling in the wind.

You will always miss the lives you're still living—now—you playing guitar / singing, to the cottonwoods, feet in the river, the mountains cast red at sunset. (You writing this on a TV tray table in your little room / the nights are too cold.)

Your parents will never understand you. They have never seen so many stars at night; they have only known cities and suburbs and cornfield nothingness in-between. You will have to give up on the idea that they will understand / try harder to understand them.

The Temples and Towers of the Virgin will gleam rosy and resplendent for the quietest / loneliest / briefest moment of the morning. Then, the bleaching of the blue.

You will not know what to do / how to behave in civilization, in the cities. You will have to go back / stand on your hind legs / act.

The bats will swoop through the night air, softly clicking / dark shapes. They will disappear by early autumn when the rabbitbrush blooms, a sea of yellow.

You will always be looking for home. You will always be in love with too many places. You will nest in other people even though they will leave you, leave you even more forlorn, homeless, and raggedy.

(Or they will stay and love you and you will be confused.)

The flies will hover and buzz and stick to you the whole way once you've reached a certain elevation, as if you stink. As if you were rotting or dying. As if there were no other place for them to be.

You will be graceful. You will be graceless.

Some nights, you will compose the most beautiful music in your mind, right before you fall asleep. You will not know how to write it down / how to not lose.

You will estrange / be estranged / a stranger.

The elk will remain mysterious among the Douglas firs and bristlecone pines. You will never fully know what will happen / what lies in wait.

You will run around the brush all night and when day breaks and the stars fade away, you will be very lonesome. You will be very sad. You will look up at us and you will cry and yelp and yip and sing and howl at the night sky, your voice ricocheting through the canyons.

THE HOLES (IN THE STORY)

I.

I cannot account for the holes in the story (pl. stories) or recount or count (the holes) or why I keep
thinking about them & how the nights are ╱ empty of coyote songs & the predators seem too clever,
too mythical, liquid ink in the night, & the mule deer wander too
close, their mute ╱ black eyes seeking, ribs rippling under dark tufted fur. (Yes, I'm the one out pacing,
under the stars, on the phone every night.) I will leave here soon, maybe too soon,
before autumn blows through the canyon and leaves ╱ the cottonwoods yellow & the bigtooth maples
a brilliant red, before the snow in the river & snow thick across the Mojave & Great Basin.

The nights are already cold. There will be no hole where I was, where I am, the rains
will speckle up the sands, fresh, on the banks. The people here will stack up their little dams,
litter the landscapes with cairns, trample their own trails to the river as if they could

fill the holes in the stories. I too can superglue the cracks in my dry hands & walk the same

trails & think too much about going (coming) back / when I am still here.

I'm here. I haven't left yet. I just keep thinking

about the stories where you can't / look / back / maybe, at the holes, at the underworlds, at the ugly creatures you love

following you / up (back). There are punishments: you can't

jump the gun. You can't eat their food or sleep in their beds. You can't

leave. There are no stars over the cities & there will

be great mounds of earth on cold damp islands where there is no difference between dead and fairy (if I don't

read the stories / the fairy lore, I forget. I forget. I forget the code. This other life.) And yes, this

is the desert. And cricket sounds all night. And Parunuweap

gapes / a sailing. A twin canyon you never dreamed of. Here, all this time, and yet. Time stands

still (more so: this is eternal). The sun blares too bright, too

yellow. The mind plays tricks. Dreams of holes where the people climbed out of and began a life / a hole / a dream

of yucca and dried up gorges. Arroyos. Limestone awash in reds, yellows,

violets. Of barbed wire fences and pronghorn running great distances. Red rocks eroded to strange shapes. Think and stop

thinking. Stop running (there's a line (you can't see)

you cross) and you keel over / lean on your knees. Head pounding. Breath

heaved. Listen. There are distant wildfires in all directions, colossal and unimaginable, drowning
the faraway cities and everything in between in thick harsh smoke. The sun then, I heard, is a burning, half-
faded, more beautiful. A burning, sinking over the still lake. Dark ash falls like snowflakes. Listen. There are holes
in your friends' stories you can't / won't know (their lives will go on without
you—they'll stop inviting you to things). The missing

swallows everything. I checked: nothing
is following me. I will simply stumble back to the city, then to another
even bigger city, where both feel like home,
both full of holes (if there is such a thing as "full of holes"). That is

the story: nothing
I can command. (The holes in my head.) And yet, I keep thinking
if I just asked the right question, I would have all / the answers. (Where
have I been. Where I have been. What is the code. How much
can I do. How much will I miss. Can you even hear me.) Can I keep
the windows wide open at night / let the smoke trail in
and sleep (just be
here / in rapture / not tearing
myself apart).

II.

(One hole: the father, once dead, sits up—alive—on the pile of burning brush, sparks high on the crackling wind, the woods of piñon pine and juniper all bright red in flame. But why? Where is he going?)

(One hole hovers over the South Pole, colossal enough to swallow Antarctica, in late winter. The light comes through.)

(One hole: the son, the one who looks back, somehow knows he must / immediately / run away. Knows he cannot soothe his dad with any words or gesture. Cannot hold him. Cannot kiss him. Cannot shake him by the shoulders and boom, LOOK AT ME! No, look at me. *Please*. Why are you doing this.)

(One hole: (the THIS) the father, no matter how much he loves his son and the rest of his family, will chase and try to kill them, no questions asked.)

(One hole: every year the high-desert winters get shorter and warmer with less snowpack. More and more bark beetles, which are native to the area and feed on the piñon pine, survive hibernation into the spring.)

(One hole: the rest of the family—the mother and the five daughters (all women)—are punished / have to flee as well. Even though they did not look back).

(One hole: the high-desert summers are much hotter for longer spans of time. The monsoon rain patterns have changed: quick, violent thunderstorms have replaced the steady rains that thoroughly soak the soil crust.)

(One hole: Having fled all through the desert only to realize that the father could always find them by their tracks, the family decides desperately to leap into the sky. And for some reason, the family, more celestial / more powerful up in the sky, calls down to the dad and laughs at him and mocks him. Of course he is too old and tired to jump up.)

(One hole: the sun boils each day, all day long, year after year. The rainwater skims the earth in sheets.)

(One hole: the family can turn the father's arrows into tiny stars, but they cannot / will not do anything else.)

(One hole: drought-stricken, the piñon pines, even the healthy ones, will not / cannot produce the resins necessary to fight off the bark beetles. Once the beetles eat and tunnel through the bark, they destroy the trees' water-conducting tissue and burrow through the trunk and major limbs. The beetles further introduce blue-stain fungi, which grow inside and plug the trees' vascular system. Given even more potential stress from strong winds, mechanical injuries, root disease, low humidity, summer heat, and so on, the trees stand no chance.)

(One hole: it must be summer, in the hazy high of it all / dreams of water and prickly pear all dark red and salty sweet. Or is it winter, after the piñon nut harvest? Are we lying on our backs on quilts and furs, fireside, listening for the elders? Do ice floes sing in the river?)

(One hole, no questions asked.)

(One hole: slopes of dead piñon by the thousands, millions, all sun-bleached grey trunks and reddish brown leaves, blurring. It's easy to speed here.)

(One hole: it doesn't matter that when the story begins, the family is very happy together. The fact that the dad even says, I am very happy.)

(One hole: the fire from the first scene must have burned down the juniper and piñon woods around the brush pile. And the fire leapt to the thick fields of cheatgrass already dried to a phosphorescent yellow among the old man sage and rabbitbrush in the valleys. And the fire blazed through the long, flat stretches of chaparral and old-burn areas. Through the acres and acres of dead piñon forests. Through the wildflowers, locoweed, ferns, Gambel oak, ponderosa, spruce, and Douglas fir on the rim.)

(One hole: the story ends focused solely on the dad, his longing and loneliness, his cries and howls, after his family turns him into a wild coyote. It is unclear whether, once turned into stars, the family A) can no longer speak, B) they choose not to, C) they, cold and bright, no longer have feelings, or D) their own grief in response to the dad's grief was considered unimportant to the narrator and, thus, the story.)

(One hole: the fire burns all summer, in its wake all char. Ash falls like snow. Whether people consider fire a part of the natural cycle determines whether or not they will try to fight it / keep it cornered.)

(One hole: there must have been volcanoes here, a time when molten lava mantled the earth, bubbling bright and sumac. The lava hardened to rough hewn patched dark, to hills of black hunks, sharp rocks clinking underfoot. The pioneers would not cross such lands.)

(One hole: The story does not mention the fire / where it goes. The fire swallows the earth. The smoke engulfs the sky. The time for us to be out—alive—drinking is when the sun, all soft red, sinks through the haze.)

(One hole: There are no coyotes left in the canyon. They moved to New York and ride the subways all night, jittery, ears perked to the clanking, the rush of wind through the tunnels. They find the bits of blue-mussel strewn shore under the steel bridges and watch the black water and the lights, listening.)

(One hole, so it was, and so it was so.)

When I sang "Moon River" in that silent film
Had I really made a sound when they called action?

—FATHER JOHN MISTY, "Only Son of the Ladiesman"

Have you lost enough?
Have another drink, get lost in us
This is how we get notorious

—LORDE, "Perfect Places"

THE CITY I CALL

This is the city of schmaltz. Of dead novels and unfinished memoirs. Of being drunk, whole-bottle-of-cheap-red-wine-chugged drunk, in the arboretum at dusk.

This is the city we weren't talking to each other / boarded the wrong train headed east on the big Island. This was just the beginning.

This is the city I was born in. This is the city where my family lives.

This is the city of sun-bleached choked grass, of bright red bougainvillea spilling over fences. Of succulents and plumeria and beardy palm trees. Of cycads and air plants.

This is the city of Elvis living forever. Of limping around with a sprained ankle. Of climbing the red sandstone fins and standing like warriors for Greg taking our pictures.

In all the cities, I just want to be a musician. I didn't want to want to write (this).

My dad says he'll never live far from the cities. He tells me this practically every time I go home.

Of ennui. Of furniture stores with spectacular 3D signs covered in light bulbs. Of Mexican bakeries and wig shops and vintage cowboy boot boutiques.

In this city, DH reminds me: this city / this love / this life / *it chooses you.*

Of cheap seats. Of spinning plates. Of heartbreak. Of flashing expired bus-transfer tickets with your best smile. Of singing loud / not loud enough over the crowds in the street.

This is the city I am the master
of writing long (sad) songs.

Of Extended Stay America hotels, singing in the stairwells. Of running along up-Spag aka Spagnoli Road, lined with dead trees and trash thrown out of cars. Of black snow and some guy yelling *CHINK* from his car.

This is the city of exile. Sanctuary. A last resort. An embarrassment (of riches, spoils, fools in love, etc.).

In this city, I dreamed of the other city. Even though I had never been there before. I dreamed of it. Wrote of it. Dreamed of it. Until it was mine and no one else could ever go to it or fuck it up.

Of dry towels, of palm trees, of In-N-Out Burger stands, of Venezuelan arepas, of crispy-duck curry in strip malls, of slot machines in the airport, of men and women in hoodies squinting and freezing on the Strip flicking out the business cards of strippers.

This is the city of my friends, my dei ex machinis (pl.). Of falling in love with everyone (and no one).

In one city, I think about how I approach description, whether I really only use metaphor or lists (synecdoche). If my writing is simply one big fat list, undone.

Wherever I have gone, the blues run the game

This is the city of survival. I don't mean the noble kind.

This is a '*driving song,*' *the hood of the car eating up the white stripes on the road in the night. Thlp thlp thlp thlp thlp.*

This is the city I stopped listening to folk music. I listened to The National, nonstop. The National. The National. The National. A fog in my brain in another city in the fish market / violence / violet / I couldn't even walk straight.

This is the city of hurricane dark. Of the smack of buildings left etched dark towers and low red emergency lights. Of giant piles of sand and trash strewn in the streets. Of torn up boardwalk and Kelsey and Gina holding hands walking toward the beach against the dark cloudy sky.

I can't keep track of the cities my friends live in. Even if it's the same city. I can't keep track of my friends.

Of Phosphorescent and his songs spun out of the Mexican desert. Of the lead singer of fun. singing about missing his parents and his voice on the vocoder going all crazy. Of Bright Eyes and their traveling songs. Of Taylor Swift and her music videos where her curly hair is perfect and she is gorgeous.

This is the city of boarding the early island ferry with all the other marathon runners, bundled up in all the clothes we would throw away. Of standing on the bow in the rain watching the Statue of Liberty, the stockyards, fade into the fog. Of everyone finding a seat and sitting as long as we could.

A long time ago, while other members of the Canidae family traveled over land bridges to other continents and evolved into other species, coyote is the one who stayed, making it a truly North American dog.

In one city, it is winter. Or is it summer.

Where everything is detail.

Of walking into a room, the only / token Asian. Of watching movies starring only white people.

I write you a story / *but it loses its thread* / *and all of my witnesses* / *Keep turning up, keep turning up dead*

This is the city you can't drive to, heading southwest on the I-15, after three or four in the afternoon—the sun will blind you—a sheer wall of light. And still,

it will emerge

from the alien desert (not

like a mirage, but a summer fair, past

midsummer, a sickle moon, a half-dollar pulled from behind your ear. It was there the whole time. The puke in the street. The castles and palaces, cute and gemlike from far away).

In this city, it took a week to not sweat so much when running, two months to feel "normal." Then, who knows how long to stop noticing things—all these things all too familiar.

This is the city for the very young and very poor and very rich. For the hopeful and hopeless.

This is the country of torn-up, abandoned railroad lines. Of white people in Victorian dresses and suits driving their Ford Model Ts to the national parks, wading in the hot springs, sitting in the amphitheater watching the grizzly bears feasting on loads of trash.

Of moving every autumn, of white rooms and corners to be emptied and filled, of boxes and boxes of things we own.

This is the city where all my selves—my whole life—buzz / tremble / shake / crash / ache / exist all at once. No neat stack of clean plates balanced on a waiter's hand. No. Nothing is that simple.

      The National sings, *I live in a city sorrow built*. I hear you, I say (in my head).

            This is the city you came back to after walking 2,650 miles straight across the country. This was before I met you.

Of one downtown city block completely industrial and empty (*Ten years ago it was like the Walking Dead*, the taxi driver said. *You would never ever walk around here at night.*) and then the next one bustling with hip trendy restaurants and cafés and bars and music and white people laughing smiling everywhere dressed like summer.

A writer acquaintance who I haven't seen in months, maybe a year, asks, where in the world have you been? But I hear: where in the world have you been *hiding*?

            Where the winds hit heavy on the borderline

My mom was born in another city across the ocean, a city, the streets, I can never fully remember even if I have been there so many times to see Pau Pau and everybody. This is how tall the concrete buildings are, how tightly packed together, strung with laundry out of the windows, the double-decker buses and signs and neon and tarp and bamboo scaffolding everywhere. This is the smell of the old neighborhoods and the gai si, the blood, the trash, the swimming humidity. These are the people the people the people. This is the Cantonese, loud and in tune, sharp as a knife, a cleaver. These are the trees here, banyan, their rope roots dangling, reaching, from the branches. The plumeria flowers like sunny-side up eggs. The green papayas raying out from the trunk. These are the silent, dark island mountains tangled in jungle, smothered in sloped concrete. This is the beach where the ragged wild dogs run along the waves, the little junks and squid and fish disappear, and the water is always warm.

Of rot and blooms of black mold. Of the ceiling, once waterlogged, bulging and peeling off brown. Of rats scurrying and dying in the walls. Of pale grey sunlight. Of Catty crying outside my door. Of Denver bolting loose and me chasing her crazy through traffic, calling and calling

This is the city where people don't look you in the eye.

In one city, I never feel well enough to write (if to write means feeling well).

They go wild

In one city, nothing is quite as satisfying as prying out gnarled root balls of Himalayan blackberry from the soil. Sometimes it takes your whole body weight, a rocking. Sometimes the root ball is the size of a human heart. A stubborn fist.

Of hustling. Of busking. Of form rejection letters. Of laughing about being poor and eating beans from a can. Of Alex coming back only in the summers and saying I was the most gangster gangster he knew.

This is the city. This is the Chinatown where my dad grew up with his parents and six siblings, he the fifth born. This, the cramped tiny apartment above a grocery store a block from the school. This, the ice from fish tossed in the street and the fire escape and the window he must have looked out of a million times. These, the dreams of jello and vanilla sandwich cookies and condensed milk in cans and gum and cavities and his dad, my Ye-Ye, walking back late from nights at the restaurant (I imagine him walking up a great hill wearing a jaunty hat but these are the flatlands) home, smelling like onions and garlic and grenadine. And running up to him, this must have been the dream: to be the favorite, the most beloved.

This is the city where people love to hear themselves talk. They pat themselves on the back and eat their organic vegan gluten-free locally sourced marionberry cake.

I want to hurry home to you
        put on a slow dumb show for you and crack you up
                so you can put a blue ribbon on my brain
                        God, I'm very very frightening

I'll overdo it

This city will beat you up and knock you down and write its number on your hand.

      This is a city spun round with volcanoes. This is a city carved out by giant glaciers and big hills were sluiced down.

This is the city of poetry and *poultry under the stairs*. Of drinking wine and laughing and reading through the whole *The Importance of Being Earnest* with all our friends at the old craftsman. Of coming back and finding everyone gone / busy / distant / awkward / uninterested / unresponsive. They have outgrown you now. They don't know how to talk to you.

The coloring of coyotes depends on whether they live in the desert—lighter, sandy, tan—or the forest/higher elevations— dark grey and black. At their underbelly, soft white fur.

This is the city of the feeling I don't fit in with anyone / anywhere. The reasons I don't know if I know.

      Where the rivers freeze and summers end

Of African men selling knit scarves and hats on the street. Of yellow shawarma stands. Of rats in the tracks and express trains shuttering fast over rats through rusting caged innards.

This is the city of staring down the barrel of a gun. Of picking the last meat clean off the bone.

> *My family lives in a different state.*
> *If you don't know what to make of it, then we will not relate.*

Of precociousness. Of preciousness. Of delicate poets. Of bullshit. Of buying coffee just to loiter in cafés.

In this city, I want to talk about Race. But how? Where do I start? What if I'm always just surrounded by white people? What if I'm the only angry one?

In one city, these boys (not men) asked me why I was so sad sometimes. As if there was / could be / should be a reason. As if they can't handle me.

Of Netflix brainlessness. Of Monday-night lines at the grocery store. Of constant dehumidifier hum. Of home-cooked meals and eating with our knees touching.

This is the city where I'm in love with the trains—their silver shot sides and green submarine windows, how suburbia blurs on the express. And I'm running for it. The train. I'm always late / running / sweating like crazy. I don't look at the clock. I make the world rush and blur. I'm time traveling.

Of tiny tacos and the best horchata, all swirly with cinnamon. Of the best bulgogi and kalbi sizzling on the plate. Of sitting in traffic for hours, reggaetón on every radio station. Of watching skateboarders plunging over concrete.

In one city, I stop writing. Then I start. Then I stop. Then I start. I stop. I should be looking for a job. I should be making a difference. I should be giving back to the community. I should be devoting myself to a third-world country. Or something. Something better.

Of Bob Dylan. Johnny Cash. First Aid Kit. Queen. Rihanna's "Diamonds." The Head and the Heart. Mumford & Sons. Maroon 5's "Daylight." Of Monsters and Men. Macklemore. "Wagon Wheel." Edward Sharpe and the Magnetic Zeros. Phillip Phillips's "Home." Of my teammates singing Hoodie Allen singing about having no faith in this city. Of The Lumineers and me singing my own cover / crying, *Dead Sea / you told me I was like the Dead Sea / don't ever sink when you are with me—*

This is the city where we have to keep talking or we lose each other (in the dark, in the city, in my mind).

Of magical thinking. Of breaking down in Pike Place and hiding in the upstairs nook of the anarchist bookstore. Of hobo prophets. Of slinging coffee. Of not reading for long spells. Then, of reading too many books at once and forgetting everything.

See for me that her hair's hanging down | It curls and falls all down her chest

This is the city the winter lingers on forever.

Of encores, or rather, conscious déjà vu | repetitions. Of starving. Of raging. Of singing loud my coyote heart. Of standing like a dancer at streetlights, waiting at the crosswalk—I am not a dancer but look at my potential to *be* a dancer—

Of scooping gallons of water from the rain barrel to dump on the tomato plants in the garden. Of sweaty bike rides to the library. Of mopping the kitchen floor. Of mowing the lawn wearing clunky earmuffs. Of picking apple pears from the trees. Of standing on a ladder and painting the shed a pale yellow with a dark red trim. Of burying dead pets under the gingko tree.

This is the city of I love you / I don't love you / at least, I love you but not in the same way / as before / I mean / hold me / hold me close, but / don't kiss me on the mouth / I'll kiss you on the cheek / kiss me on the cheek / we can agree to this / because I love someone else more / because I'll leave you for her / not you / nothing is about you / I'll leave you / I'll kiss you on the mouth then / when you don't expect it / don't expect anything / except / I leave you / empty

In this city, everyone I ever meet asks me if I'm going to go back. Back to the city I came from.

In one city, in the art museum, in a small dark grey carpeted room, I sat in the corner with my back against the wall and watched The National perform "Sorrow" live, on repeat, nonstop in another city in a room in another art museum. I don't know where in the six hours of "Sorrow" they were, where in the middle of the middle. I don't know how I long I watched, how many times they played "Sorrow" when I was there, how was this madness even working, why hadn't I been there earlier, did I really have anywhere else to be, could I stay forever—

In this city, white wealthy hipsters are moving into the Mexican and Puerto Rican neighborhoods and calling it theirs. This is (what) our generation (wants), they must think.

This is the city where Owen was my brother and the stories are all one story. The story of us playing hooky and he got a tattoo on his arm and we wandered through the cemetery and jumped the chain-link fence to escape and I sliced my palm open and I still have the scar. The story of running through the dusk to the end of Beards Fork Holler, where the old coal mine opened like a cave in the dark, where the stream began. The story of me always wanting to wear his grey sweater and I told him so. The story of us always talking about all the songs we loved and the people we loved who didn't love us / back.

This is the city I think—no—*believe* beggars can't be choosers. And this is the city of too many choices and too many of them
stupid.

In one city, Audrey Hepburn, in a long black dress and gloves and pearls and diamonds, gets the mean reds and stands outside the Tiffany's on Fifth Avenue before it opens, pulls a doughnut from a white paper bag and takes a small bite. She keeps her telephone in a suitcase and an orange nameless cat she calls Cat or a no-name slob. She always talks about marrying rich people. On the fire escape outside of her room, she plays a little guitar and sings "Moon River" and a writer (male/white/blond/boring) listens and falls in love with her.

This is the city the Southern Paiute elders remember—the little houses and dirt streets and hills and magnificent desert. Before it was a city, relentless, before everything.

In one city, in a hard rain, we stumbled nearly tripped soaking tired down steep stairs into the belly of a tiny jazz bar to listen, our boots all wet. It was the thing to do / the only place to be that night, in a line of many and so few nights.

In this city, I was taught (no one had to teach me) to crave normality / whiteness. (Sometimes) I (still) can't shake it.

Of droopy topped hemlocks. Of feathery cedars. Of snowberries, salal, Indian plum, Oregon grape, sword ferns, fiddlehead ferns. Of huckleberry, wild blueberries, salmonberries, trailing blackberries. Of wood sorrel. Of skunk cabbage. Of vanilla leaf and bear grass.

We can't talk about the coyote without talking about human western expansion/settler history. I mean, talking about the destruction. The genocide. I mean, those pictures of hunters with hundreds / thousands / millions (some indeterminate number) of the dead / in pelts.

Then I don't know how to talk anymore.

In one city, Keegan buys me sunflowers and fruit out-of-season to cheer me up, and I don't tell him I love him enough.

This is the city of looking. Looking around. Looking down. Looking up. Looking back. Looking past. Looking straight in front / at it. Roaring at it. Leaping at it. Wrenching its jaws apart with your bare hands.

That's the way I remember her best

This is me, babe. It IS me, babe. This is it.

Wherever I have gone, the blues are all the same

In one city, the temperature never seems to rise above 15 degrees. No one driving on the black-ice roads. No one out watching the fireworks at the pier. No king-crab legs, no piña coladas for New Year's.

This city / this feeling of having outgrown something / everything / everyone.

In this city, no one knows what kind of Asian American I am, whether I am whitewashed or part white. It must be my pink cheeks, my brown-black curly-wavy-straight hair, my height, my eyes. It must be the way I talk, the way I walk, something, everything. Stop speaking to me in English.

Of Denver, wet from a walk, rubbing her face on the rug to get back her scent. Of wanting to do that every single day of my life—gotta rub my face on the rug.

Please see for me if she's wearing a coat so warm / *to keep her from the howling winds*

This is the city where I was running and I just knew somehow that my parents would be around the corner, near one of the subway stops, on the footbridge over the highway. And there they were. My mom leaping out to hug me and kiss me and me stopping, half-running and all teary-eyed.

Of squeezing down the sidewalk crowded with people and stands selling fiery mangos and mango juice spinning in fountains, pineapples cut into rings, fresh pupusas slapped down to sizzle, tacos, sweaty-glassed horchata, ruedas and chicharrones, limes, bright red split watermelon full of seeds, and we're already too full.

In one city, it's easy to imagine that all my friends have a more charmed life than me. (So witty, so clever, ah haha.)

Of hunting for graffiti and murals that ooze down the walls. Of giant parking-lot towers. Of slides zipping through shark tanks. Of pirates and gambling kings. Of the Eiffel Tower, Statue of Liberty, Pyramid of Giza, a Roman palace, of everything—here—in one place. Of gondolas floating through swimming-pool-blue canals, the gondoliers singing in old Italian, the indoor sky half-dead lit blue.

This is the city I got sick as a dog. Every night we'd be nightwalking, Denver and me, running across the streets, the soft glow in the blue twilight, looking into other people's houses and wishing—the dinners on the table, the books on the shelves, the strings of fairy lights and lamplight, the laughter and tango music pouring out the doors.

Of early Thanksgiving morning standing watching the parade with the giant floats of Spider-Man and Kermit the Frog. Of climbing around the slabs of dark rock in the park. Of finding my friends and eating pancakes and waffles at the only open diner. Of lying with them on a sunny, grassy hill above the zoo until dinnertime. Of riding the El to Bird and her journalism school friends and their Friendsgiving. Of lying beside Bird in her bed with wet hair, awake, wondering about her life.

In one city, I am too suburban, not inner-city enough. I cannot say I am from this city, really. Not really.

Don't wait up for me. Please don't.

Of Irish goodbyes. Of disembodied guillotine blades floating overhead.

Of lying in the middle of a frozen lake with Q watching at the shore, judging. Of hiking through bedrock in the snowy woods with him. Of eating chiliburgers and banana cream pie in a diner silver like a bullet and watching *Silver Linings Playbook* with him, watching his face watching. Of listening to him play the harmonica in a drafty campground hall shed, huge and echoey like a hunk of a sunken ship.

I don't think about the gray wolves, their extirpation, how that gray-wolf hole makes it just right, just so, for the coyotes.

The only good thing (idea) the human robot (robot human?) told me was that I was (like) the Bosporus Bridge. At once, two continents. At once, poet and prose writer and musician. At once, city girl and savage. At once, fey and ridiculous, mundanely alive. It was/is alright to be both(?).

This is when you get angry, Pickles. Don't be sad, be angry, said DH, in an email. *Give yourself over to rage.*

This is the city I slept in the freezing, smoky, windowless room of a dead man. Everything in his room—the clothes in the closet, the baseball caps on the dresser, the posters, the books—were as he left it months before.

Like the Dead Sea
You told me I was like the Dead Sea

. . .

Nicest words you ever said to me
Honey, can't you see
I was born to be, be your Dead Sea?

Of Arby's. Of Potbelly's original Italian sandwich on wheat, all the toppings no mustard please. Of gyros from the corner store, extra pitas wrapped in foil. Of Italian beef sandwiches drenched in au jus. Of (burnt down) Nuevo León tostadas (carne asada and refried beans on the crispiest tortilla and the fine sprinkle of cotija cheese) and Cantón Regio kebabs and paletas de mamey and mango. Of Indian lunch buffet, all the chicken tikka masala and melty minty pista kulfi. Of Arabic food on giant silver platters and coffee in tiny silver cups in an empty restaurant at Ramadan.

This is the city of my vanity and I am all the more vain.

In one city, the English ivy snarls itself thick and heavy around trees and sends them toppling down in the wind.

This is the city where my friends spent most of their nights at the one bar a fifteen-minute walk from the ship, sometimes with some of the crew. There was no need to say the reason.

In one city, I cry every time I'm in the airport with my parents. I watch *Frances Ha* and get teary-eyed when Frances says goodbye to her parents at the airport.

Of rusty skeletal steel towers and train bridges and train tracks and water towers. Of boxcars and concrete walls laced with graffiti. Of an empty Printers Row. Of the meatpacking district—all the barns, stalls, cows, pigs, hay, blood—underfoot, pressed flat clean.

This is the city I can't stop singing / thinking / writing about the song "Oh Shenandoah," how Shenandoah is a river / place / person / chief / a mythical Virginia. Of all the contradictions.

> Oh Shenandoah, I long to hear you.
> Oh Shenandoah, I long to see you.
> Oh Shenandoah, I could not deceive you.
> Oh Shenandoah, I'm bound to leave you.
> Oh Shenandoah, I love your daughter.
> Look away, rolling river!
> I take her across the open water—
>
> Away, oh, bound away, across the wide Missouri!

In one city, you feel you have lost something. A certain sweetness and light.

The word *worry*, originally, in old hunting terms, meant to seize—like a dog, like a wolf, like a coyote—a smaller animal by the back of the neck and swing and strangle and thrash the animal until it dies. The word *worry* we have turned on ourselves / internalized / this thrashing of the mind.

In this sky, in the cities, only the Big Dipper, Cassiopeia, and Orion shine through the mute winter nights.

She was once a true love of mine

This is the city of broken bones. Of limping along the water's edge, through the arboretum at the end of autumn, over the highway, the very last runner of the marathon—alone, phoneless, cold, snot-nosed, wrapped in space blankets—while all the roads open back up to cars, the water booths close down, the sun sets, and everyone thinks there's something wrong (with me). Of taking painkillers every hour or so. Of the feeling of parting the air / the sea with every small step / the pain. The feeling I had to finish or die, unloved, ashamed. The feeling I could not stop if I tried.

1872	Mark Twain's semi-autobiographical travelogue, *Roughing It*, denigrates the coyote as a *long, slim, sick and sorry-looking skeleton, with a gray wolfskin stretched over it* and *always poor, out of luck, and friendless*.
1920	An article in *Scientific American* labeled the coyote as "the Original Bolshevik."
1940s	Hunters employed by the federal government labeled coyotes a public enemy on par with Nazi Germany.

In this city, I'm trying to laugh at myself / not take myself so seriously / write things that are fun/funny. But I'm not laughing.

This is the city where Kelsey and Sav could have been twins, good cop/bad cop. Kelsey was the one who tripped on the stairs at the strip club and got a gash on her forehead and bled on Sav's Jayhawks jacket, but no stranger could get the story right. No one could tell them apart.

Of straightening my hair with another girl's straightener and strolling off the ship and into the seagulled morning and onto a bus and onto the subway and into the city just as the clouds burned away.

This is the city where I sing Townes Van Zandt. Sing *if I needed you, would you come to me / would you swim the seas / for to ease my pain?*

Of bleached out driftwood stacked into forts. Of kelp bulbs tangled and strewn on the beach, detached from their underwater forests. Of ferries crossing the silent waters on the hour and glowing like ghost ships.

This is the city Andrew Bird sings about, the city where the music (everything) started (for him), the city at night. He keeps singing to me, *come back / come back to the City of Light.* Come back to Pulaski, the bridges over highways at night, all the red and white lights in streaks. Come back to Maxwell Street, keep the car running and locked, Dad will buy the Polish sausages and homeless men will try to sell him white socks and roses. The sausages will be dripping with caramelized onions, the fries will be greasy and limp, the grape soda will make you choke, but it will be so good. It will be perfect.

Of asking anyone older, "What was your life like when you were twenty-eight (or twenty-nine)? What did you worry about? Who were your friends? What did you do for fun? What did you listen to? What did you eat?"

In this city, I sing along with The Lumineers singing, *When my hands begin to shake* / *When bitterness is all I taste* / *And my car won't stop* / *'cause I cut the brakes* / *I hold on to a hope in my fate* (but I hear: *I hold on to a* hole in my face).

Or I've parked so far away I don't remember how many blocks I've been walking with my head bent down in the wind. If it's Keegan and me and we've reached the oldest church in the city left standing after the great fire, it's warm inside and the stained glass is dark and we are close and our cheeks are feverish.

In this city, my mom keeps chickens in her garden now that we have left. The chickens go into their little plastic playhouse coop at dusk, and then my mom locks the door. She is afraid of the raccoons, foxes, and coyotes. She says I worry her sick.

This is the city people are always slouching / looking down at their phones (and I wonder if anyone is living / alive / if I am no better).

Of watching the sunrise over the distant city from the ship's deck with Alex. Of keeping the gulls from stealing our lunches packed in white paper bags. Of nights staring at the black water under the dock, hearing Beirut's "The Rip Tide"—the rocking piano, the long, lonely trumpet solo.

Even today, I can't say the reasons out loud (because they are dumb) but there are songs
they come on and I run out of things to say:

> The Head and the Heart – "Rivers and Roads"
> Edward Sharpe and the Magnetic Zeros – "Home"
> Calvin Harris – "Feel So Close"
> Maroon 5 – "She Will Be Loved"

Of blue mountains in the distance. Of lichen in green scaly sheets. Of highways that sound like rivers.

This city is my playground. My black snow mountains in the strip-mall parking lots. My suburbs blank sameness to drive
through and forget. My high-end grocery stores filled with all kinds of cheeses in rounds, beautiful fruit, muesli, Icelandic
chocolate, French vegetable soaps. I can go as long as I want, as far as I want, but I have to be home for dinner.

This was once the city of stalking. Night after night. Of biking through the nightdark in dark clothes, through hailstorms.
The hail half-melted in the soft grass, the stinging of cheeks. Of staring up at lit windows and pressing / not pressing buzzers.
Of lying in wait. Of trying to get the right angle. Of wishing / trying so hard to be
seen / not seen.

This is the city a man loaded with twenty-three guns—twelve of them semiautomatic rifles—checks into a casino hotel, goes up to his suite, smashes out the windows, and guns down a country music festival across the street. He kills fifty-eight and wounds 851 people. Then he kills himself. He leaves no notes / reasons.

In less than a hundred years, the Bureau of Biological Survey, a division of the US Department of Agriculture, working with private, local, and state control campaigns, destroyed approximately twenty million coyotes.

In one city, I told Owen that I listened to Johnny Cash and Bob Dylan singing "Girl from the North Country" nonstop, all the time, and at least a dozen times before I fell asleep. It was the only thing that helped. *I know*, he said. *Me too.*

This is the city. The city I feel I've been running my whole life to. I can't stay.

Then I want to tear off my skin / face / everything.

This is a country overrun with starlings. Their flocks don't make great bounding shapes over the fields here.

Of wandering around Little Tokyo while waiting to eat tonkatsu ramen (the best, if you have been in the desert forever and you have waited forever.) Of rushing through the bookstore, its book tunnels, touching everything, not reading the back of anything.

This is the city where the white kids grow up singing Woody Guthrie with their own lyrics:
This land is my land, this land ain't your land
I got a shotgun and you don't got one
If you don't get off, I'll blow your head off
This land was made for only me

This city was once a true love of mine.

Of hobbling about on crutches, on and off buses, up and down staircases and escalators, in and out of the shower. Of crutchwalking over Catty stumbling about with a cloth cone around his neck. Of capital moods, a rainless anomaly winter of eternal high-angled sun. Of learning to walk again, each step a falling.

In this city, it is so easy to stop busking / showing your face. Too easy to disappear with your music. Of course there's nothing like busking to make you feel like a dog.

In one city, the streets and subways are filled with Black and brown people—yes, I will be blunt—and I feel safe. I feel happy.

This is the city of runny noses wiped on sleeves.

The National sings, *If I stay here, trouble will find me*. I hear you, I hear you, I say (in my head, in my head).

In this city, I don't cut my hair. I keep my long stretched-out curls, all my bleached dead cells. I keep myself intact.

This is the city that DH and I always meet around Christmas / New Year's / his birthday at the Publican, slurp down their soup of the day with oyster crackers, chow down on a Reuben sandwich with tiny pickles on the side. Then we jump on the Blue Line, go to our favorite nerdy café, and wander down Milwaukee. The rest is not so set (but we have to make it happen).

Of worrying about my mom and dad walking slowly down the Strip too far from the car and having to walk all the way back. Of driving in circles around the casinos, late, hungry. Of rushing through airport security together and me crying when we have to split up, go to different gates, different cities.

Unlike wolves who travel and hunt in packs (a collective of unrelated wolves), coyotes are solitary creatures. If they do come together, it is in the late spring through summer to mate and form a family unit (a mother, father, current pups, older pups, and maybe an unrelated "aunt" or "uncle"). When summer ends and the current pups are old enough to hunt on their own, the family unit disperses until the next summer.

In this city, the poem / nothing can be contained right—it sprawls / spills / wrenches from the edges. It glistens
on the bar, wet and amber and sticky.

Rivers and roads / *Rivers and roads* / *Rivers till I reach you*

In this city, the ship I once lived on is docked too faraway / inaccessible / mythical (in the hood, the bad part of town, across the water, on the way to nowhere). There is no sane reason to visit it.

In this city, I spend my whole life waiting for summer.

Of Arcade Fire. Laura Marling. Sharon Van Etten. The Lone Bellow. "Youth" by Daughter. The Antlers singing, *we're not scared of making caves or finding food for him to eat* / *we're terrified of one another,* / *terrified of what that means.*

In one city, my mom tells me she wishes I were there to help her and my dad with the Great Migration aka the moving of all the indoor plants from the sunroom to outside for the summer, back inside for the winter. She wishes I were there to help clean the house, bring things to donate at Goodwill, pick up groceries, roast the cha siu, learn to cook better, go out with my siblings, swing on the swings, read in the living room, stay for longer, etc. etc.

1.   This is the city where Owen dashed from shop to shop at the Christmas market to find Alex a little leather bag the color of a fawn for her birthday and she would hate it and never carry it.

2.   This is the city where I spent a very cold day hunting out a copy of Rilke's *Letters to a Young Poet* and a loaf of German bread covered in poppy seeds from an authentic German bakery to give to Q (who was living far from the city, out in freezing, snowy northern country) to say I'm sorry for being mad at you, forgive me. (Instead of

fuck you, FUCK YOU, why am I even giving you gifts or talking to you again, why am I so fucking stupid, why can't I admit that I have every right to be angry, why can't I stay angry for long, why do I feel like I have to make everyone else happy before me—they don't fucking deserve anything—why can't I follow my instincts, why can't I just say something anything, why am I so pathetic,

always kicking myself to death—).

Q would eat all of the bread by himself and lose the book before reading it.

Of people rolling off the beach selling scrap art and vintage trash spread out on dirty blankets on the sandy sidewalk. Of walking over bridges over canals and swan boats to ogle at big rich houses with their giant windows and holey-leafed philodendrons and tables set for summery dinner parties. Of the salty air and the silvery beach and the squinting bright blue sky and sun stretching on forever.

This is the city of singing "Riptide" by Vance Joy because it sounds like the West, a cowboy song, the only song I seem to know and remember, a song about running into the rushing water. *And they come unstuck—*

This is the city where all that's left of the human robot (robot human?) I loved are

1) The lines of an Auden poem he loved:

> *I am the solitude that asks and promises nothing:*
> *That is how I shall set you free. There is no love;*
> *There are only the various envies, all of them sad.*

2) The (unshakeable) feeling of feeling too raggedy to wait for him / to be the one waiting for him / to be the one for him.

3) An email that read: *Look here, someone still loves you. Now, look away! Look away!*

This is the city that tries with all its might to keep you from writing / singing / running. (Or it is indifferent(?).)

> *And I'd be saying that you*
> *You're always holding on to stars*
> *I think they're better from afar*
> *'Cause no one is gonna save us*

This is the city I began from. I drove to the desert for the first time. I got out of the car at every vista point, took a million pictures, puked all over the landscape the heartsick.

This is the city Keegan and I hiked through a young forest then climbed through knee-deep snow, glaring and bright, up a mountain. We dug our toes into the inclines / stabbed our way up with trekking poles. At the summit, we sat on the snow and ate mac and cheese and squinted in our sunglasses, looking back at the city—blue, small, beautiful.

This city is / faraway / the heartland / the rhineland / the rind.

Of my lovebirds weathering the cold winters in the sunroom, some dying each time, their feet curled up. Of scraping ice off windshields, clumsily, with thick gloves on. Of Christmas lights strung along gutters long into March.

This is me: riding into this city in the back of a big black van with the AC blasting, Joshua trees whirring through the gorges, I'm the one sealed behind tinted glass. I'm the one escaping. I'm the one listening to The National singing *I'll still destroy you* with all its drum machine kicks and bright high sounds and the feeling of sleepwalking off a cliff.

The members of coyote family units keep in touch with their own group howls.

This is the city of Adri, Adri who shakes the sand from her hair and clothes and goes off to teach. Of lemon trees in the courtyard. Of a beach wild with scraggly red brush and seagrass and barnacles and bouncing high up in the cold waves. Of a garden full of forests and paintings and libraries and huge agaves and blue cacti. Of a sunset from the observatory that stretched forever red and orange and violet across the hazy sky.

Of heaping pastrami on rye sandwiches. Of ramen and pork belly sliders. Of plain slice pizza. Of Taiwanese hand-pulled noodles covered in spicy lamb. Of Nepalese curries in little piles on a round silver tray.

In this city, in an old email from Marcela in Brazil, I learn that the way I interpret saudades is incorrect. And still, it makes no difference to me. Ainda eu tenho saudades de tudo mundo. They are my strange legless cloud sheep, and I their keeper. Their wool does not keep me (or anyone else) warm.

And they go wild

Of sliding down snowy mountains on our butts on old therm-a-rests. The city of gravity.

Of singing The Head and the Heart's "Heaven Go Easy On Me" with Alison and Dylan at the old house: *All these things are rushing by* / *All things must end, darling* / *All these things are rushing by—*

I know this city on rollerblades. I know the feel of sidewalk cracks, the metallic ridges on bridges. How to step up and down at curbs, how to part the crowd around me.

In this city, in our home city, Justin and I meet up for the first time in the after. He kisses me on the top of my head, the only friend to ever do that. I touch his springy hair. We wander the streets. *It's so weird to see you here*, I say. *It's like we've escaped from the zoo!* We laugh and laugh and laugh.

This is the city where (my) fiction died / it is dead
in my hands, and my friends demand to know why.
I demand to know why we are
too busy for each other / what fiction
are you telling me
am I telling you.

> *Spin me round just to pin me down on the corner of this strange bed*
> *I'll be home in a little while*
> *Lover, I'll be home*

> This is the city where the backwards river and the lake like an ocean freeze over and the waves are
> white spikes.

This is the city we talk about leaving—but never do.

In some states, you can turn in a pair of coyote ears (how would that work? the hacking with a knife, the dead earless coyote) for a bounty (do you mean treasure?).

In that particular story, Audrey Hepburn gets out of jail and tries to run away from this city to Brazil. The writer tries to stop her. He says, *I love you, you belong to me!* Instead of *you belong* with *me.* Even she says, *No. People don't belong to people . . . I'm like Cat here, a no-name slob. We belong to nobody, and nobody belongs to us. We don't even belong to each other.* Yet, in the movie, in this city, she's wrong. He wins: he gets the girl. He captures her.

The last I heard of Owen—this is after I last saw him, an assistant funeral director in a heavy large grey suit in another city, sweating, hardly looking at me—he ran away to the desert and joined a conservation crew there and met the love of his life and followed her everywhere—

Look away, rolling river!

One mouse—the one from the country or the city—turns to the other and says, *One of us has lost touch. Lost* (our) *touch.*

Of running past Ashley's old house by the high school track, looking up at her windows, wishing she is / knowing she is not home. Just me (always going back always running the same route).

In this city, I thought I had an old soul. I mean, that's what they said and I believed them. They said I was going to be famous. They said, *Man, you've got a set of pipes. You can really blow.*

This is the Era of the "Super Coyote." When one (you?) randomly kills that many coyotes, one (you?) selects for coyotes that are smarter and bolder. Hence, the Super Coyote. Moreover, once one (you?) disturbs coyotes' established social structures, one (you?) gets suborder males rushing to spread out, multiply, and stake out their own territories with more pups. Reduce the number of coyotes in a given area by 70 percent one summer and they will be back to their original numbers by the next.

I like / don't like thinking we are the last of our kind.

Somewhere, in this city, Ye-Ye and Ma-Ma owned and ran a Chinese American restaurant for so many years. It was where my dad and his siblings cooked and waited tables and washed dishes. It was open on Thanksgiving and Christmas and New Year's. It was where my parents first met. I know almost nothing about it. I don't know if it's still standing. I don't know how many American cousins I have.

In this city, we fight in the train station. We always seem to fight in train stations. We fight until the sun sets and all that's left are gold streaks across the sky. Almost all of the shops in the quarter that feel like old Mexico are closed, but we still make it into one. We look at the ceramics, alebrijes, sombreros, piggy banks, santito candles and bracelets. We eat tamales with salsa verde and walk down the cobblestone streets. We slip into the night.

Of buses like grasshoppers plunging through tunnels. Of rain smell and the slick wet sound of streets under wheels. Of mudrooms and wet coats and clothes draped all over the furniture and opened umbrellas in the bathtub.

In this city / this city / this city,
I can't run / run away from it / everything.

This is the city where Gina snuck out after curfew, slept with a shipmate, got pregnant, and left us. She would not listen to us. She would move back to her hometown in the desert. She would have a boy and name him William Carlos and put him up for adoption. She would only talk to Kelsey, call her *mama*, tell her about her other mamas.

Did you know that if, when we met, you didn't help me move random craigslist furniture with your truck, if I didn't wrap you in scotch tape, if you didn't catch up to me after the show, if we didn't eat a whole bag of chips and salsa at the willow beach together, if we didn't try / hold / consider (the stars), we would have lost each other?

Of moving all the crap off my dad's record player and breaking out the secondhand records. Of summertime spinning Frankie Valli and the Four Seasons and Hall & Oates and Johnny Cash's *At Folsom Prison*. Of wintertime with Johnny, again, and Bob Dylan.

In cities, coyotes have learned to observe traffic patterns to figure out how and when to cross roads safely. They have been figuring out ways to deal with whatever we've done to the landscape.

Of swinging on the weathered swings my whole life, all through the seasons, dreaming up stories against my feet against the trees against the sky.

This is the city of my mom's beautiful food (the secret: spit and love). She tries to teach us to cook, but she moves and talks too fast and doesn't let us touch or cut anything. *Too slow, so inefficient*, she says and snatches the knife away.

In this city, you seem so good / you are goodness / you are untouched (untouchable) / you don't seem to miss me the same way as I miss you. I think I am too much / I am too savage / too crazy / I want to be that dog with its face out the car driving fast window with the wind. That dog. Can I be that. Can I be good. Can I measure it. The good. The crazy. The missing. Can the missing not be like chasing your own tail, like living with saudades, too much (negative) space.

This is the city they hound you. This city will gut you, kick you in the back of your knees.

Of soft blankets of starry mosses. Of foxglove and talus slopes. Of large flecks of pale green lichen like antlers fallen from the trees. Of glacial floured lakes all aquamarine. Of Douglas firs and western red cedars. Of islands too muddy in winter. Of bog country and drumlins and filled in tidal flats.

Of falling in love with tahini and halvah, halvah in colorful rounds by the pound, halvah sneaked into chocolate croissants. Of goats' milk ice cream piled with crushed halvah and drizzled with tahini.

This is the city I know ╱ can never get lost in, blindfolded, in the dark, wearing sunglasses.

This is the city of not fitting in well with other Chinese. The reasons—me not speaking Mandarin, not able to read or write, not nouveau riche, my Hong Kong mom, my ABC dad, my height, my freedom, my bad Cantonese, my English, my being too juk sing, too American, my silence, their disappointment, the fear the fear the fear—are not so simple.

And they go wild

In one city, I forget. I forget so much. Maybe on purpose. And I can't tell if the forgetting is a blessing, or a curse.

Of standing with you at the corner of Canal and Bowery in the Chinatown,
so I could replace the image of Q and I standing in the same place years before,
so you and I could be the sweethearts in The Lumineers song.

Coyote must kill

> sheep, cattle, and other large livestock if all its usual small
> mammal prey—the cottontails, jackrabbits, prairie dogs,
> rats, mice, etc.—are scarce or have disappeared
> completely due to trapping, killing,
> and/or habitat destruction due
> to human development(s) due to a need(?) due
> to a fear that coyote, if left unchecked (uncontrolled?
> unmanned?) will multiply and spread out ad
> infinitum over the land mangy rabid
> starving killing whatever it can
> snatch, all the big
> game that humans want to kill
> to feel something, to kill it before it can kill you,
> to kill to understand because there
> are

those who don't understand.

In this city, when we (only with you) fight, I have learned to stand up and speak—even if my vocal cords are being torn out.

Of a dying Chinatown (already the third one) and a gentrified historically Black neighborhood. Of hobos sleeping under the highway in fancy REI tents. Of stars in the hills.

This is the country walking backwards
into whiteness
                              erasure
                                                            denial.

Of listening to Elephant Revival's "Down to the Sea" on repeat:

I found her in an ocean from a puddle of a town nearly drowned
But no you couldn't keep her down
The city it saved her, at least until it claimed her
She misplaced her life in a strange arrangement of days
Through the silver city haze

And oh, so begins the frantic violin—

In this city, so far away, I wonder if I can, if I'm allowed to, talk about the Southern Paiutes. If they will think I am taking / assuming / speaking for them when I don't mean to. If anyone can speak for another person / people / peoples. If I myself can say or do anything without always representing me / my family / my people / my race carrying my earth / my sky.

I love you when you're singing that song and / *I got a lump in my throat 'cause* / *you're gonna sing the words wrong*

Of pulling on a white tyvek hazmat suit over our uniforms, blurry goggles and filter masks over our faces, gardening gloves over latex gloves, hard hats on top, and marching into strangers' homes with hammers and crowbars. Of carrying all their things—so wet and moldy and broken and unidentifiable— to the curb. Of tearing up floorboards, balancing on the narrow supports left behind. Of scrubbing clouds of mold—dark, powdery, and fine—from the scaffolding beams in the dark.

Today 80,000 coyotes are (still) killed annually via aerial gunning.

The highway signs say we're close, but I don't read those things anymore. I never trusted my own eyes.

This is not my city.

This is the black hole (city? cities?) where so many of my old friends fell into. Or maybe it's that they think I've fallen into it. Or maybe, I believe too much (too little? not enough?) in this, this tightrope walking over the dark abyss, this tin can on a string, this white noise, this music, this moon.

In one city, you run and run and no one is chasing you anymore. Even if you want it. Want them to want you.

Rivers till I reach you

This is the city I thought I would move to when I was little. I loved the name.

This is the city, the only city where I feel *I made it*. Made it to Central Park. Here I am running on pavement between the sycamores and crowded barricades. Soggy red leaves beneath my feet. The cheering nonstop, anonymous, wondrous. I am dead tired and sick and teary-eyed and soaked to the skin and happy and still running.

The legends tell it that, at the end of time, Coyote will be the last one standing on this earth. But Coyote is social and does not like to be left alone. We can walk together or go our separate ways. The choice is ours.

It's the way the light
comes down.

Of dancing and running through thunderstorms, drenched. Of odd green skies and tornado dreams.

In one city, food will save you. The reading of food magazines and recipes and gathering the ingredients. The carnitas and mole negro. Lotus root chicken soup. Niku udon, curry udon. Thai green curry with little eggplants and enoki mushrooms. Kalbi ribs. Kimchi fried rice. Tomato and fennel soup. Spicy cumin hand-pulled noodles. French lemon yogurt cake. The beating of eggs with chopsticks. The stir-frying and sizzle. The roasting. The slow cooking and simmering until the windows start sweating.

This is the city of stars. Of Edward Hopper paintings and that certain green slant of light. Of Old Hollywood and instrumental big brass band sound and winding mansioned boulevards and choked up highways.

Of waiting for hours for the train in the freezing cold, a foot of snow covering the tracks. Of a faraway Chinese New Year festival I would never make it to. Of my teammates swinging by in the guvvy, fishtailing, taking me to eat sandwiches and watch a dumb comedy at the movies, and none of it was Chinese and all of it was.

Well, I have faded in the dark
So don't you ever kiss me
Don't you wish on me
Why can't you see that no one's gonna save us?

This is the city I drove back to from the desert, the city I began from. And so much of the way—after the hilly country and the great silver arch of one city—there are big colorful hot-air balloons floating over the greenest cornfields and wind turbines. And I am better. I am clean. I show my parents all the pictures so they could know where I been.

(If you needed me, I would come to you. I would swim the seas for to ease your pain)

I'm still in love with this city. All of its trees: the willows on the water's edge, the red of vine-maple leaves, the madrona bark peeling to reveal green heart. The bright twigs in its hair. The mossy stones and the smell of rain. The lighthouse perched on the foggy sea. We both know it won't/wouldn't work out, but we still stare at each other from across the room.

Near this city, at a Thai restaurant, my mom and dad (crying, making me cry) tell me the reason.
The reason why they're like this / why we're like this / why it has always been, always is, always will be
just us, this family, in this city faraway across the world / we are stars / why I shouldn't be angry, even
if things seem unfair, they aren't / why my parents would do anything to help my siblings and me, anything, everything:

We had no one else in the world.
And this is the consequence in the beginning in the city I was born:
We had no one else to depend on but ourselves.

Of one splendid mad afternoon running around with Denver in the overgrown backyard bathed in soft golden light / covered
in dog shit. Of Catty, timid on the step, gnawing on tulip leaves.

And they go wild

In this city, when I finish writing / this, I will be done with it. Everything. I will be spent. And the words will fall away to
just this / the music. And I will keep nightwalking. I will climb out of the canyon into the desert, into the smoky whistling
wind. And I will keep nightwalking. I will stand at the edge of the salt sea, shivering, dripping, shake myself off like a dog.
And I will keep nightwalking.

I can look up. Look away.   I can go home.

I can go live—

NOTES

The first epigraph is from Joan Didion's essay, "On Morality," published in *Slouching Towards Bethlehem* (1965).

The second epigraph and many other quotes from Clifford Jake can be found in *Southern Paiute: A Portrait* (2010) by Logan Hebner with photography by Michael Plyler.

"Why Coyote Looks Up When He Howls" is adapted from William R. Palmer's retelling in *Why the North Star Stands Still and Other Indian Legends* (1978) and another version in LaVan Martineau's *Southern Paiutes: Legends, Lore, Language and Lineage* (1992). I am trying to be a better ally to Indigenous and Native people, and I acknowledge that this Southern Paiute winter's tale is not mine to tell. I also acknowledge that this story has most likely been changed and is no longer true to its original form through the many insidious ways of settler colonization, and I do not wish to perpetuate this harm. Though I hope in my retelling of and conversations with this story, my respect, gratitude, and love comes through. Thank you.

NOTES FOR "THE CITY I CALL"

All life and natural history facts on coyotes come from various books and articles for my research conducted at Zion National Park for my evening program on coyotes. Much of the same information can be found in many different sources.

The bit on a "'driving song,' the hood of the car eating up the white stripes on the road in the night. Thlp thlp thlp thlp thlp," comes from an *Independent* review of The National's *Sleep Well Beast* by Christopher Hooton. The song he's referring to is the title track "Sleep Well Beast."

The bit on the word "worry" and its etymology draws from an excerpt from Adam Phillip's *On Kissing, Tickling, and Being Bored: Psychoanalytic Essays on the Unexamined Life* (1998). The artist Ann Hamilton featured this particular excerpt in her *the common S E N S E* exhibit at the Henry Art Museum from October 11, 2014 to April 26, 2015 (where I first encountered it).

The bit on Audrey Hepburn and "that particular story" refers to the film *Breakfast at Tiffany's* (1961).

The bit on The National playing their song "Sorrow" for six hours straight refers to "A Lot of Sorrow," a six-hour endurance art video released in 2014, created by Icelandic multimedia artist Ragnar Kjartansson and The National. The video documents and draws all of its footage from The National's original six-hour performance in the VW Dome at MoMA PS1 in front of a live audience in May 2013. Within those six hours, "Sorrow" was performed 103 times. "A Lot of Sorrow" played at the Art Institute of Chicago from June 24 to October 23, 2016.

The W. H. Auden poem mentioned is "In Praise of Limestone" (1948).

The following is a list of all the songs and their respective lyrics I quoted or referenced in "The city I call":

Andrew Bird, "Pulaski at Night." *I Want to See Pulaski at Night*, Grimsey Records, 2013.
I write you a story / but it loses its thread / and all of my witnesses / Keep turning up, keep turning up dead
Come back to Chicago / City of Light

The Antlers, "Bear." *Hospice*, Frenchkiss, 2009.
We're not scared of making caves or finding food for him to eat
We're terrified of one another, terrified of what that means

Beirut, "The Rip Tide." *The Rip Tide*, Pompeii Records, 2011.

Bob Dylan and Johnny Cash, "Girl from the North Country." *Nashville Skyline*, Columbia, 1969.

She was once a true love of mine
Please see for me if she's wearing a coat so warm / to keep her from the howling winds
Where the winds hit heavy on the borderline
Where the rivers freeze and summers end
See for me that her hair hangs long / It curls and falls all down her chest
That's the way I remember her best

Bright Eyes, "Old Soul Song (For the New World Order)." *I'm Wide Awake, It's Morning*, Saddle Creek, 2005.

They go wild
And they go wild

Elephant Revival, "Down to the Sea." *These Changing Skies*, Itz Evolving Records, 2013.

I found her in an ocean from a puddle of a town nearly drowned
But no you couldn't keep her down
The city it saved her, at least until it claimed her
She misplaced her life in a strange arrangement of days
Through the silver city haze

fun., "Stars." *Some Nights*, Fueled by Ramen, 2012.

> *And I'd be saying that you*
> *You're always holding on to stars*
> *I think they're better from afar*
> *'Cause no one is gonna save us*
>
> *Well, I have faded in the dark*
> *So don't you ever kiss me*
> *Don't you wish on me*
> *Why can't you see that no one's gonna save us?*

The Head and the Heart, "Rivers and Roads." *The Head and the Heart*, Sub Pop, 2011.

> *My family lives in a different state*
> *If you don't know what to make of it,*
> *then we will not relate*
>
> *Rivers and roads, rivers and roads*
> *Rivers till I reach you*

The Head and the Heart, "Heaven Go Easy On Me." *The Head and the Heart*, Sub Pop, 2011.

> *All these things are rushing by*
> *All things must end, darling*

Jackson C. Frank, "Blues Run the Game." *Jackson C. Frank*, Columbia/EMI & Castle Music, 1965.

> *Wherever I have gone / The blues run the game*
> *Wherever I have gone / The blues are all the same*

The Lumineers, "Dead Sea." *The Lumineers*, Dualtone, 2012.

> *Like the Dead Sea*
> *You told me I was like the Dead Sea*
> *Nicest words you ever said to me*
> *Honey, can't you see*
> *I was born to be, be your Dead Sea?*

The Lumineers, "Morning Song." *The Lumineers*, Dualtone, 2012.

> *When my hands begin to shake*
> *When bitterness is all I taste*
> *And my car won't stop*
> *'Cause I cut the brakes*
> *I hold on to a hope in my fate*

The Lumineers, "Stubborn Love." *The Lumineers*, Dualtone, 2012.

> *The highway signs say we're close*
> *But I don't read those things anymore*
> *I never trusted my own eyes*

The unnamed The Lumineers song is "Ho Hey." *The Lumineers*, Dualtone, 2012.

Mumford & Sons, "Home." 2011.

> *Spin me round just to pin me down on the corner of this strange bed*
> *And I'll be home in a little while*
> *Lover, I'll be home*

The National, "I'll Still Destroy You," *Sleep Well Beast*, 4AD, 2017.

The National, "Sea of Love." *Trouble Will Find Me*, 4AD, 2013.

> *If I stay here, trouble will find me*

The National, "Slow Show." *Boxer*, Beggars Banquet, 2007.

> *I want to hurry home to you*
> *put on a slow dumb show for you and crack you up*
> *so you can put a blue ribbon on my brain*
> *God, I'm very very frightening*
> *I'll overdo it*

The National, "Sorrow." *High Violet*, 4AD, 2010.

> *I live in a city sorrow built*

"Oh Shenandoah," a "traditional American folk song of uncertain origin, dating to the early nineteenth century," according to Wikipedia. The version and lyrics that I know best are from Trampled By Turtles's "Oh Shenandoah."

> *Oh Shenandoah, I long to hear you.*
> *Oh Shenandoah, I long to see you.*
> *Oh Shenandoah, I could not deceive you.*
> *Oh Shenandoah, I'm bound to leave you.*
> *Oh Shenandoah, I love your daughter.*
> *Look away, rolling river!*
> *I take her across the open water—*
> *Away, oh, bound away, across the wide Missouri!*

Townes Van Zandt, "If I Needed You." *The Late Great Townes Van Zandt*, Poppy, 1972.

> *If I needed you,*
> *Would you come to me*
> *Would you swim the seas*
> *For to ease my pain?*
>
> *If you needed me,*
> *I would come to you*
> *I would swim the seas*
> *For to ease your pain*

Vance Joy, "Riptide." *Dream Your Life Away*, Liberation Music, 2014.

    And they come unstuck

    I love you when you're singing that song and ╱I got a lump in my throat 'cause ╱you're gonna sing
        the words wrong

ACKNOWLEDGEMENTS

My deepest appreciation goes to the family, friends, teachers, ghosts, ancestors, and mentors that these poems were written for, written with, written toward. I am made better for having listened to you, for your wisdom, for your kindness.

Thank you to Bruce Rutledge and Yuko Enomoto at Chin Music Press for taking a chance on this sideways book with all its hoops to jump through, and for all your hard work in publishing the beautiful books you do. Thank you to Dan D Shafer for your brilliant design work. And muchísimas gracias to publicist and dear friend Adriana Campoy, always, for your grace and support.

Thank you to Dorena Martineau, cultural resources director of the Paiute Indian Tribe of Utah, for patiently listening to me trying/failing to explain this book and for helping check over my retelling of "Why Coyote Looks Up When He Howls." Thank you to the Southern Paiute People for this beautiful winter's tale, for your knowledge and stewardship of the high desert.

Thank you to the artists and music quoted here. Thank you to my poetry and prose ancestors. To my fairy godmother, Michael Madonick: RIP and thank you for believing in my kid voice and me since day one. Thank you to Madonick's Children—I have learned the most about poetry from you.

Thank you to my Big Booty Bitches AmeriCorps family for that insane, unforgettable year. I will always appreciate your heart, courage, and service.

Thank you to Zion National Park and the Zion National Park Forever Project. Thank you to the past, present, and future stewards of our public and natural lands. Thank you to Zoe Wiesel for adopting me as soon as I arrived to Zion, taking care of me, and sharing your art and love for Zion. Thank you to Angelina Guerra, LuAnn Gifford, Toni Tracy, and Emerson Hammerslag for your friendship and cheering me up. Thank you to Sunny Lee for picking up my call, jumping in your pickup truck, saving me from the top of that mesa, and feeding me artichoke pizza after.

Thank you to Nick Banach aka Dickhead/DH, Miranda Schmidt, Audie Shushan, Sarah Lindenbaum, Abi Pollokoff, and Mary McCormack aka Spicerack for your love and writing through all the years. Thank you to Greg Bem and Marlene Schmidt for the big dreams and adventures. Thank you to Devashree Dave, June Chiu aka Spoon, and Tim Taft for your inspiration and friendship and sharing your food with me. Thank you to Lynn Stansbury and John Hess, always, for supporting the rebel and Romantic in me. Thank you to Alison Stagner and Dylan Moir for your joy and music, for always welcoming me home and making me laugh. Thank you to Catty and Denver for waiting at the door and licking my face.

And thank you to my dearest Keegan O'Rourke for letting this old mooch into your heart and for sharing this crazy life with me.

Lastly, a big, big thank you to my mom and dad; my siblings Randy, Alison, and D; my sister-in-law Jenny; and my Pau Pau. Thank you for all the love and food and home, for this life, for always being there for me through thick and thin and the many marathons. I could not do this without you. I am so grateful for you every day.

Colophon

This poetry collection was first published in the late-arriving
spring of 2023 in Seattle, Washington. The primary font is
Californian FB, a custom creation of American type designer
Frederic Goudy for the University of California Press in 1938.
It is supported by the sturdier sans serif font Trade Gothic,
designed by Jackson Burke in 1948, who coincidentally attended
UC Berkeley around the time of Californian FB's release.

FIRST PRINTING / EDITION OF 1,500